Friendly [ ] Hotels of Wales   1998

First impression: November 1998

© Copyright Chris Thomas/Y Lolfa Cyf. 1998

ISBN: 0 86243 424 6

Printed, published and bound in Wales by:
Y Lolfa Cyf., Talybont, Ceredigion SY24 5AP
e-mail ylolfa@ylolfa.com
internet http://www.ylolfa.com/
phone (01970) 832 304
fax 832 782
isdn 832 813

Friendly Fishing Hotels of Wales

CHRIS THOMAS

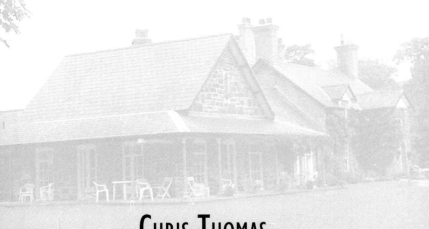

yLolfa

Contents

Introduction

To more than a few of us, one of the sadder consequences of social engineering and change during the latter part of the twentieth century is the inexorable decline in the fortunes of the traditional British rural public house.

Take a trip in the countryside in any direction and you will see them; silent, lifeless, many with "For Sale" signs attached more in a forlorn hope than any real anticipation of attracting a new tenant. Once-valued centres of social interchange, bustling with life and laughter on a Saturday night, they sit there, as some have sat for hundreds of years, with blank windows rattling in the breeze, their mouldering tap-rooms filled with the ghosts of lost conversations.

Several valid reasons have been cited for this loss of part of our social heritage. Among them are the dreaded breathalyser, an increase in home entertainment, the price of beers and spirits. There are many other causes, and all have contributed to the decline in some way or other – the breathalyser more than most, some might say. Certainly the continuing existence of most urban hostelries, particularly those in town and city centres where the use of a car is not so necessary, would tend to reinforce this assertion.

Yet very many country pubs still survive, thank goodness. Generally, it will be found that these are the ones which have introduced something more to offer their customers than just a place to pour beer down their necks. Those which began offering meals in the early days of the decline had a head start, as did those which could supply accommodation. Others installed televisions, gaming machines, pool tables, canned music, the alien-named Karaoke machine. Love 'em or hate 'em, few would seriously dispute that without 'em the rural boozer could well be in danger of total extinction.

And not only the pubs. Many residential hotels, particularly those in the country far from the motorways and trunk roads, are threatened by the headlong pace of our ever-changing requirements. Not so dependent upon the sale of alcoholic drinks, true, but subject to ever-increasing expenses, great seasonal variations and vulnerable to the expanding popularity of alternative holiday destinations.

Self-catering holidays in caravans, cottages and farmhouses are preferred by many on grounds of financial restriction and the freedom to arrange their own times for meals, etc. Touring caravans, package holidays abroad, trunk-road motels – for every person who opts for one of these it is one less customer for a traditional hotel. Look along any seaside resort promenade and observe how many former hotels and guest houses have been converted into holiday flats, DSS boarding houses or simply closed down entirely.

Fortunately, most rural hotels have escaped this fate, due in a large part to the fact that there are still a lot of folk who appreciate the quiet of the countryside away from the rowdy fleshpots. And, like the remaining rural pubs, a large number owe their continuing survival to the extras over and above a bed for the night that they can provide.

Peace and quiet has already been mentioned. Other services can include a swimming pool, tennis, golf, croquet, horse riding …

… and fishing.

And this last is what this little book is about. The fishing hotels; more specifically the fishing hotels of Wales: those which can offer a stretch of river or a lake for guests to pursue their angling aspirations.

Their diversity is capable of satisfying any requirement demanded by today's discerning customers. From snug roadside taverns letting a few rooms to virtual stately homes with up to sixty bedrooms – the range is broad. Tariffs will naturally vary with the grandeur of the appointments.

But why, you may reasonably ask, should you stay at a fishing hotel when you could rent a self-catering cottage, go for bed and breakfast and travel round the club waters or sleep under the stars with a backpack?

Well, apart from the matter of financial expenditure, which can be rather acute for some of us, the benefits gained invariably outweigh the possible extra cash layout.

For a start, in these pages will be found many hotels which provide *free* fishing for their guests, so there will be no need to fork out extra from a restricted budget for day or weekly tickets on club waters. Furthermore, in most cases the fishing will be almost outside the door, thus enabling those last few and highly important twilight casts to be made just a matter of yards from shelter, warmth and beer. No need to tramp over the fields back to the car in the dark and drive miles to where you are staying if you don't want to.

Then there is the matter of good relationships with the proprietor. Those who run hotels catering for anglers will have become accustomed to their idiosyncrasies, their single-minded devotion to their craft and their muddy boots. Hotels unused to these little peccadilloes may be inclined to a certain diffidence, if not badly-concealed hostility, towards such otherwise innocent guests.

Like-minded company is important, too. Other anglers will usually be in the immediate vicinity and you will have the opportunity to share in the modest and often highly original untruths common to all the angler species. There can be few more satisfying ways of passing the latter part of an evening than to quaff a pint or three with others of the same ilk as yourself in a corner of a comfortable bar with no problem about driving home, good food on hand which you will not have to cook yourself and a fresh, clean bed to crawl into which somebody else has made up for you. At such times friendships are made as well as arrangements to fish in company the following day.

Besides, those staying in hotels amenable to night fishing are recommended to have company on hand when striving to tempt a sea trout or salmon in the pitch dark. On the rockier rivers it can be a comfort to know there is somebody close by when a false step could possibly lead to a sprained ankle, a ducking or worse. Two torches are always better than one, too. Ever tried landing a fifteen pound salmon from a bare-rock rapid holding a straining, bucking rod in one hand, the landing net in the other and a heavy torch clamped between a twin-set of rapidly-loosening false teeth?

It isn't easy!

But for any angler looking for a place to rest his weary head after a hard day by the river, and enjoy the services of a well-run hotel, the fishing offered will be the deciding factor. This is what the author will attempt to describe in the following pages.

Rivers come in all sizes and types. Wales can supply the lot. As most anglers will agree, the size of a river does not necessarily bear any relationship to the quality of fishing it can provide. Little streams can often be prolific compared to the wider watercourses they run into, if only because they are easier to cover. Trout will be the main quarry here – and grayling in many of the North Wales rivers.

The larger rivers, of course, can add migratory fish -- the noble salmon and the sea trout (locally known as sewin). A lot of hotel waters will contain these active, silvery immigrants from the sea. Some, like those on the lower Teifi, Usk, Wye and Dee have runs of large spring fish while all enjoy the main influx from about June onwards in years of "normal" rainfall.

Some of the hotels listed, although not owning their own waters, can arrange local fishing. There is usually an extra charge for this – not all guests wish to fish, it must be remembered, and it is manifestly unfair to expect them to subsidise those who do. A few, however, will make no charge even if the guest stays only a single night. There are no fixed rules about this so careful scrutiny of the text about each individual hotel is essential. All facts are correct at the time of writing, and references to left and right banks respectively can be orientated correctly by the observer facing *downstream.*

It must not be forgotten that the grayling, an exciting sporting fish, is classed as "coarse" and is subject to the same close season as the roach, perch, bream, etc. It can therefore be pursued during the winter months. As both hotel tariffs and riverbank competition tend to be much less at that time, a winter break – or even a full week's holiday – should be seriously considered.

The choice of the most important venues and description of hotel and fishing is necessarily subjective. Having fished on all the rivers mentioned (and most of the others in Wales) the author feels he is amply qualified to comment on their characters and prospects for the visiting angler.

But fish are fickle creatures, as every angler will know. Any river, apparently dead one day, can boil with fish on the following with no obvious difference in either weather or water conditions. With this fact in mind, the potential visitor is strongly advised not to restrict him- (or her-) self to a single set of tackle. Take all sorts, unless specifically forbidden on the hotel's water. Wet and dry fly, spinner, bait, anything which will enable you to adapt to changing conditions. There may be a drought in Birmingham at the same time as flood warnings are issued in Wales. Hotels which specify a fly-only rule are identified in the text.

It is a regrettable fact that, in common with so many other parts of the country, facilities for the severely disabled are the exception rather than the rule. Unless specifically stated to the contrary, it can be assumed that a hotel is unable to cater for those who rely on the use of a wheelchair to get around. Those which do are listed in the section of the book entitled "Facilities and Concessions".

In mitigation, it must be said that hotels owning traditional fishing rights tend to be older buildings which do not lend themselves readily to conversion. Neither, with just a few exceptions, are the majority of fishing holdings suitable for wheelchairs. Those who are able to get around despite being partially disabled are in a far better position since most of the hotels mentioned either adjoin the river or are within a short walk. It will be found that most of the waters listed have good and easy bank access.

But safety becomes more important when in the water. A lot of Welsh rivers are rocky and deep. Wading can be rather hazardous during high summer when that ghastly green algae spreads itself over the river bed. If you possess studded waders, take them in preference to the rubber or felt-soled variety (or both types – along with a puncture repair kit). A self-inflating safety jacket can sometimes be a sensible precaution too, especially when fishing the larger and more powerful rivers like the Dee, Teifi, Towy and Wye.

It is also a good idea to take along a large, extending landing net when in pursuit of salmon or sea trout because gently shelving pebble beaches are somewhat of a rarity on many Welsh rivers. And if you want to do any night fishing alone, don't take one torch – take *two;* one powerful one for doing the business and a small pocket lamp for when a bulb blows in the big one during the darkest part of the night. A couple of spare bulbs wouldn't go amiss, either.

The book is split into five sections, each of which is arranged in alphabetical order. The major and better-known hotels are dealt with in the first, then the others which cater for anglers but which may not have so much water or only have preferential access to local fishing. It must not be assumed that these latter are lacking in any way whatsoever; the facilities are invariably good and the fishing often superb. They are every bit as worthwhile for the fishing and can often have lower tariffs than the bigger establishments. Following this is a short list of establishments without their own water but which welcome the angling fraternity and are happy to arrange local fishing for them.

The fourth section is a series of lists giving quick reference to concessions not always on offer; where dogs are allowed to stay, for instance. All hotels are able to supply packed meals for a full day on the water and nearly all can supply real ale for the terminally thirsty.

The final section is a list which matches the Welsh rivers with the hotels having access to them. If you wish to try a particular river above all others, this will give you the names of the hotels with fishing at which to book a room. Details of them can then be checked in the other four sections. It may be noticed that a particular hotel will appear under several river headings. This is because it will have access to more than one stretch of water.

For those who have not yet experienced the friendly hospitality and wealth of excellent angling that Welsh fishing hotels have to offer, it is hoped that this little book will encourage the reader to give at least a few of them the chance to prove their worth. But before moving on to the individual hotels, a few dismal words of warning may be in order.

During the research undertaken to compile the information contained herein, use was made of data going back as far as the 1960's. To the author's dismay, a significant number of fishing hotels had ceased trading since those days with the result that their riparian holdings had been sold off to wealthy private individuals, syndicates or angling clubs which do not issue day tickets. *So much* formerly accessible water is now effectively out of the reach of the visitor – and even the locals, in many cases.

But such is the inevitable result of today's changing customs. As said at the beginning, not only the rural pubs and residential hotels but even those with such a valued asset as first-class fishing have been affected. Unless those remaining are supported by anglers, the numbers available will inexorably decrease to the detriment of all. Nothing can be taken for granted in these frenetic days.

So please, anglers, support our remaining fishing hotels. Not only in Wales – help to retain those struggling to make a living in Scotland, Ireland and England too. One day they may not be there for us all to enjoy.

The loss will be ours. And we will all have to share some of the blame.

Hotels specialising in angling

Each of the following hotels listed is
well-known to, and patronised by,
Welsh anglers.

What better recommendation could there be?

Aber-nant Lake Hotel

The spa towns of the Irfon valley were once renowned for the properties of their mineral wells, the most famous being at Llanwrtyd Wells – "the smallest town in Britain". During Victorian times *this* was the place to be seen when "taking the waters". Sulphur and chalybeate springs were the "in" thing at that time – good for the scurvy, it was alleged. Although these same mineral wells are not so much in favour of late, their heyday ensured that several big hotels were built locally to accommodate the large influx of visitors.

The best known is the Aber-nant Lake Hotel (WTB 3 crowns).

An imposing and airy building standing on the eastern side of the town, the hotel offers 59 bedrooms, all en suite. Located just off the A483 between Llandovery and Builth

Wells (and close to the Mid-Wales Line railway station), it is in a quiet position with open views over well-kept parkland to the Eppynt mountains beyond.

Both river and lake fishing can be enjoyed here. The river holding is a 1½ mile stretch of left bank on the Irfon – a beautiful stream noted for its grayling. But don't forget the fine brown trout and late-season salmon! Access is easy.

This is one of the few fishing hotels which *can* cater for severely disabled anglers, both at the premises and for lake fishing. The 9 acre lake is regularly stocked with trout well over half a pound and there are pike and plentiful coarse fish of several species. There are no boats at the time of writing but this will hopefully be addressed in the near future. Casting platforms are planned for the extra convenience of wheelchair users and there is vehicular access to the lake.

Fishing is free to guests, with no minimum stay required. Dogs are permitted and real ale is supplied in the large and comfortable lounge bar.

The Manager, Aber-nant Lake Hotel, Llanwrtyd Wells, Powys, LD5 4RR.
Tel: 01591 610250 *Fax:* 01591 610648

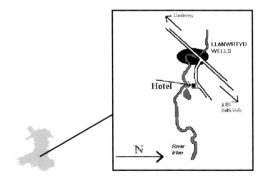

Bell Hotel

The A40 is an ancient thoroughfare; once a drover's track, then a coaching route which was subsequently converted into the trunk road of today. The Bell Hotel (WTB 2 crowns) at Glangrwyney is said to have originally been built as a rest home for the monks who were building the nearby Llanthony Abbey before being used as a coaching inn during the 17th century.

Standing alongside the A40 in a little village just north of the interesting market town of Abergavenny, it can offer 4 double bedrooms, all en suite and all recently refurbished to a high standard. The premises are well patronised for the quality of the home-cooked food.

There is a comfortable oak-beamed lounge area and a snug "locals" bar furnished in traditional style. Dogs are permitted in the bar where real ale is served, but not in the hotel.

The fishing, although a relatively short stretch, has a very good reputation locally. A short, level walk of about 300 yards will bring one to the bottom of the beat which comprises approximately 450 yards of right bank. Located in the lower middle reaches of the famous River Usk, there is plenty of water to explore and it fishes best in relatively low conditions when good rises can be expected in the afternoon and evening. The whole stretch is packed with wild brownies up to 2 lb and over and the regulating dam in the head-waters often supplies a refreshing rise in water level during times of drought.

Fly only is the rule for both trout and the salmon which enter the Usk from early in the year. There is even the chance of a sea trout from June or July on. Fishing is an extra modest charge on accommodation. Since only 4 rods (1 per person per day) are allowed, and permits can also be issued to those not actually staying at the hotel, it is as well to reserve your rod in advance when booking a room.

The Bell Hotel, Glangrwyney, nr Crickhowell, Powys, NP8 IEH.
Tel: 01873 810247.

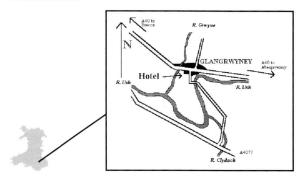

Brigands Inn

Situated at Mallwyd on the A470 trunk road between Machynlleth and Dolgellau is the well-known hostelry of the Brigands Inn, a coaching inn since the 15th century and specialising in angling for the last hundred-plus years. It was named in memory of the notorious red-haired bandits (mentioned in George Borrow's *Wild Wales*) who terrorised the area long ago and sometimes used the building as a base for their nefarious operations.

Rest easy! The bandit gang broke up long ago, their descendants now fully integrated into society – except perhaps for those who chose careers as Income Tax or VAT inspectors. The beautiful surrounding valley today bears no sign of its violent history; indeed, the Brigands Inn is as friendly a place as you could find.

Besides its 13 rooms (7 en suite) and six kennels for the comfort of guest's dogs, the listed premises provides a well-stocked bar and tackle shop.

A fascinating mixture of streamy runs, rapids, gorges and deep pools, the fishing holdings run to about 2½ miles either bank of the Dovey and one of its major tributaries, the Cleifion. There are 12 named holding pools (and plenty more which are unnamed), many bordered by a clear bank – a boon when stalking sea trout at night. Further concessions are available on 8 miles of the Twymyn a few miles down the valley.

The Dovey, queen of rivers! Probably the best sea trout river in the UK and subject to occasional roaring spates which bring up salmon and sea trout in great numbers. But it is not a good brown trout venue. Instead, the hotel can offer excellent trouting on two lakes, complete with boating facilities, in the mountains not far away.

The fishing is an extra charge and only offered to resident guests. Fly only is preferred unless the water is high, but bait anglers are adequately catered for. Night fishing is a speciality. A map of the hotel waters is on display in the lounge bar.

The Brigands Inn, Mallwyd, Machynlleth, Powys, SY20 9HJ.
Tel: 01650 531208. *Fax:* 01650 531460.

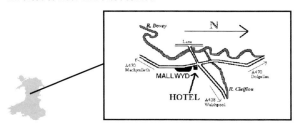

Bryn Howel Hotel & Restaurant

This elegant red-brick building, constructed in 1896 by a local brick manufacturer, bears superlative testimony to the high quality of his product. In 1963 it was transformed into the top hotel and restaurant in the area with a 3-star AA and RAC rating and is one of only five restaurants in Wales to boast 3 AA rosettes for very fine food prepared with considerable flair, imagination and originality.

There are 36 bedrooms, all with en suite bathrooms, colour TV and attractive views. Located among green meadows in the beautiful Vale of Llangollen, the privately-owned hotel offers visitors an extremely comprehensive package of services and amenities to suit all tastes. A sauna, solarium and accommodation for under 16-year-old children sharing with parents are available free of charge. A few rooms are suitable for disabled guests confined to wheelchairs. Others are designated for dogs to stay at the discretion of management.

Private fishing is offered over a full five miles of the River Dee – a fine, varied stretch with many named salmon holding pools, long fast runs and rippling flats. A perfect mix of water allowing successful fishing in flood or drought. The regulating dams of Brenig and Celyn often give clear-water mini-spates at low summer levels.

The fishing is free to guests however long they stay. Fly, spinning and bait. Not only can a fisherman's picnic be provided if you are reluctant to leave the river, but the hotel will cook and serve a hot meal on the riverbank if you wish. And when you catch that specimen, you can have it served up for dinner that very same day!

Further activities which the hotel arranges on request include canoeing, hot air balloon rides, pony-trekking, golf, rock climbing, mountain biking and canal trips. Those who prefer less physical activities can patronise the fine oak-panelled lounge bar with its fascinating ceiling and fireplace to sample what the well-stocked cellar has to offer.

Bryn Howel Hotel and Restaurant, Llangollen, Wrexham, LL20 7UW.
Tel: 01978 860331. *Fax:* 01978 860119.

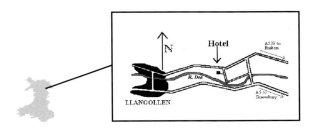

Caer Beris Manor

On the outskirts of the market town of Builth Wells (home to the famous Royal Welsh Show) stands the picturesque, half-timbered Caer Beris Manor. It is reached from the A483 by a tree-lined driveway beside the River Irfon. The 3-star and WTB 4-crowns hotel occupies the summit of a wooded knoll almost surrounded by the river. A neat central courtyard allows access to this grand old building which contains 22 bedrooms, all with en suite bath and shower. Dogs are welcome to accompany guests.

First-class free fishing may be enjoyed by guests on two rivers – the Irfon and the Wye. Nearly 1,000 yards left bank of the Irfon is owned by the hotel and is open to all staying there. This is a lovely stretch with fast runs and several deep pools. This is fly-only water.

The hotel also holds two rods on the local angling club's waters extending for 4 miles on the Wye (9 long salmon holding pools) with more on the Irfon. All legal methods are allowed by the club. Those wishing to fish the Wye are strongly recommended to reserve their rods in advance when booking to ensure availability.

Restricted tickets at extra charge are available on Llyn Alarch, regularly stocked with large trout and only a short walk from the hotel. This lake can be fished by those who are confined to a wheelchair and two rooms on the ground floor of the hotel are suitable for severely disabled people.

Many species of fish can be found in these waters, making this hotel eminently attractive for a winter holiday. Grayling up to 2½ lbs are everywhere. Salmon – well, the Wye is no stranger to salmon. They have been caught up to 38 lbs here. For the coarse angler there are chub (to 5 lbs), pike, dace and shad. Barbel, too. The hotel can hire rods and tackle and instruction can be arranged on a casual basis or with a gillie.

Caer Beris Manor, Garth Road, Builth Wells, Powys, LD2 3NP.
Tel: 01982 552601. *Fax:* 01982 552586.

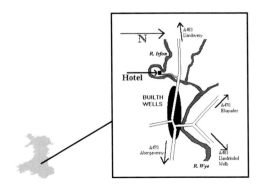

Cammarch Hotel

Llangamarch Wells is another of the famous Victorian spa towns, albeit the smallest, in the pretty valley of the River Irfon. Barium chloride was alleged to be the active ingredient of the wells here; apparently beneficial to those with heart, arthritic and rheumatoid complaints. It doesn't make things worse, anyway!

A very short walk from the Llangamarch Wells railway station on the Mid-Wales line stands the Cammarch Hotel (The Countryman's Hotel). Sandwiched in the junction between the rivers Irfon and Camarch on the edge of the village, it contains 18 bedrooms, all en suite and all with bath or shower. Recently fully refurbished to a very high standard, it is anticipated that accommodation can soon be offered to wheelchair-bound guests.

In keeping with the spirit of a true countryman's hostelry, dogs are allowed to accompany guests. A convivial bar on the ground floor provides a perfect location for anglers to swap yarns of the utmost integrity after the fish have gone off-shift.

The fishing holdings are extensive and encompass three local rivers. Fly only is the rule on all. On the Irfon, the largest, there are 3½ miles to explore for limited rods. The Camarch offers 3 miles for 3 rods and the smaller Dulas, a couple of miles downstream, allows 2 rods to fish for a mile. With a couple of other stretches, the total comes to about ten miles of very good fishing. Much of the bank is lined with ancient woodlands but there is casting space to spare under this pleasant green canopy. The fishing is available to day visitors but hotel guests always have priority.

Although the fishing is an extra charge on one's stay, guests benefit from a reduced rate on all waters. Packed meals can be provided for those who wish to spend maximum time in pursuit of the many fine brown trout, large grayling and salmon present in all the stretches.

The Cammarch Hotel, Llangamarch Wells, Powys, LD4 4BY. *Tel:* 01591 620205.

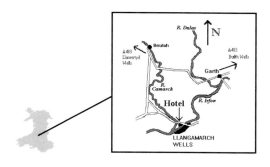

Castell Malgwyn Hotel

Standing on a low knoll amid sweeping lawns above the River Teifi, this fine 3-star hotel is approached through a pair of listed gate piers, past a gate house and down a long drive lined with grand old trees. The entrance is just off the A484 over the 18th century bridge at Llechryd about 4 miles west of Cardigan.

Fifty acres of lawn and woodland along the river are owned by the hotel, allowing many pleasant walks. There are 23 bedrooms, all en suite and all with attractive views of the grounds. The restaurant has an enviable reputation for its food and there is a large ballroom used for many functions including dinner dances for residents.

The comfortable library bar, complete with an abundance of books and an open log fire, looks out over the front grounds and croquet lawn. On the sunniest side of the building is a swimming pool for the use of guests. Dogs are welcome and are offered a complimentary menu of their own but are not allowed in the lounge or restaurant.

If you are taking children with you, please enquire about the extremely preferential rates for their accommodation.

Guests can fish 2¼ miles of the noble Teifi at no extra charge. Interesting features are the remains of an old fish weir (a good spot at any water height), a disused underground ice room and the occasional coracle still working its ancient craft in the river here. Only a couple of miles above high tide mark, the stretch enjoys early runs of salmon and sea trout. Even if they are not in the mood to be caught – which isn't often – the huge stock of brown trout, many of a very large size, provides excellent sport.

The river is easily accessible by a riverbank path with some *very* deep and powerful water in places. The immediate waterside is often steep and all baits are permitted.

The Manager, Castell Malgwyn Hotel, Llechryd, Cardigan, Ceredigion, SA43 2QU. *Tel:* 01239 682382. *Fax:* 01239 682644.

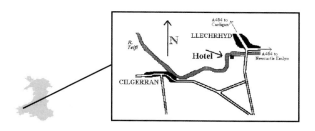

Dolaucothi Arms

Generally considered to be the most productive tributary of the famed Afon Towy, the Cothi rises high in the bleak fastness of Cerrig Cyffion. Twelve miles downstream, the clear, sparkling waters pass under the new road bridge at the tiny village of Pumsaint and here, close to the river, stands the Dolaucothi Arms.

Located about halfway between Lampeter and Llanwrda on the A482, the premises are small and cosy with a particularly convivial atmosphere. Besides the legend of the Five Saints (after whom the village is named and who each adopted their own individual pools in the river just downstream from the pub) the immediate locality is well known for its Roman gold mines which are open to the public.

The National Trust-owned premises offers 2 snug rooms to

visiting anglers (1 en suite). Real ale is on tap in the two bars and the "Butler's Kitchen" dining room supplies first-class meals.

Although not a large river, these upper reaches of the Cothi can provide superlative sport for migratory species from about July onwards in a year of average rainfall. Sea trout are the first to arrive, with the main run of salmon following on close behind. The lack of huge volumes of water, however, is more than compensated for by the length of the stretch guests are welcome to fish – eight and a half miles on the Cothi and about half a mile on the Twrch. The upper waters tend to be rather wooded and more suitable for bait fishing while the lower stretch below the village is more open, wider and easier for fly and spinner. Permits are additional to accommodation and issued to day visitors but guests benefit from a reduced rate.

Access to the river is good, night fishing can easily be arranged and packed meals provided. There are no restrictions on fishing methods; fly, worm, spinner, anything legal. Since the pub has only 2 rooms to let, early booking is essential to avoid disappointment.

The Landlord, Dolaucothi Arms, Pumsaint, Ceredigion, SA19 8UWA.
Tel: 01558 650547.

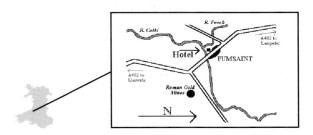

Dolmelynllyn Hall Hotel

At the southern edge of the village of Ganllwyd on the A470 just north of Dolgellau is a bridge over a picturesque little waterfall. By the side of this bridge a curving, tree-lined drive past a gate-house gives access to the well-appointed 3-star Dolmelynllyn Hall Hotel.

Standing on the upper boundary of one of the few open meadows in the middle reaches of Afon Mawddach, the hotel commands an impressive view over the deep, V-shaped and heavily wooded valley to the Coed-y-brenin forest in the east. The well-kept grounds are particularly suited to leisurely and contemplative walks. The hotel maintains a strict no-smoking policy and offers 10 excellent rooms to its visitors (all en suite). The quality of food and cellar provision is of an extremely high standard.

About 10 miles of river fishing is available to guests – free of charge if staying 4 nights or more. There are long stretches on the Mawddach, Wnion and Clywedog, both double and single bank. Llyn Cynwch, high in the mountains a couple of miles south, is also included. All provide excellent game fishing from early in the year; Afon Mawddach, the closest and just down the road, perhaps providing the best. Fishing in the two Cregennen lakes on the flanks of Cader Idris west of Dolgellau can also be arranged at an extra charge. One holds wild brown trout while the other is stocked with rainbows. A boat is available on the larger lake.

All methods of fishing approved by the River Authorities are allowed though some of the lakes are fly only. Those who fish the rivers for salmon and sea trout will be pleased to know that night fishing can be arranged for any time. Dogs are allowed to stay with guests in two of the bedrooms only, so prior booking is required to reserve this facility.

For those who require tranquillity, pleasant surroundings, gourmet feeding and first-class angling, this is the place to stay.

Mr Barkwith, Dolmelynllyn Hall Hotel, Ganllwyd, Dolgellau, Gwynedd, LL40 2HP.
Tel: 01341 440273.

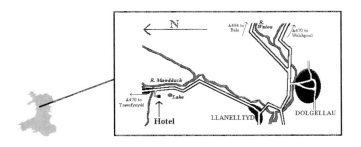

Elan Valley Hotel

The chain of artificial lakes in the Elan Valley has been well-known for many years to serious anglers and very many have stayed at the Elan Valley Hotel in order to remain as close as possible to them.

Caban Goch, the lowest reservoir, is only about 3 miles from Rhayader and is reached by the B4518 which follows the deep, narrowing valley of the River Elan. Just before the narrowest part of the valley is reached, the hotel will be seen on the right-hand side.

11 welcoming rooms are on offer, 10 of which are en suite and dogs are allowed to stay with guests by arrangement. The premises have a 3-crowns rating and approval from the WTB. There is a homely bar, a function room and an excellent restaurant.

Fishing on 1,600 acres of the three reservoirs is available at the hotel. These waters are regularly stocked with good-sized trout so there can be no possible excuse for a blank day. The banks are easily accessible, mostly; a good road following the shoreline, about half of which is wooded, the rest open. But the upper reservoir of Graig Goch (at 1,043 ft) has treeless banks all around.

Local river fishing is available on about 4 miles double bank of the upper Wye with a further mile of right bank. There are plenty of wild trout and grayling to a very respectable size here as well as salmon in the latter part of the season. Those who prefer to catch large rainbows can try their skill on Llyn Gwyn a few miles to the east, a first-class put-and-take water.

There are also about 3 miles of double bank fishing on the Afon Marteg. This is a charming little upland river well worth a try for its hard-fighting trout and some late salmon. The fishing is an extra cost to accommodation. Permitted methods of fishing vary with the waters so it is best to come equipped for all sorts when staying at this hotel.

The Elan Valley Hotel, nr Rhayader, Powys, LD6 5HN.
Tel: 01597 810448.

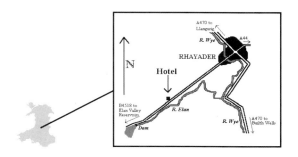

Forest Arms Hotel

The Afon Cothi, a major tributary of the famous Towy, is generally acknowledged to be one of the best sea-trout venues in the vicinity. Plenty of salmon accompany them, too. Several miles up this medium-sized spate river, the little rural village of Brechfa nestles among rolling, wooded hills and here can be found the small and hospitable Forest Arms alongside the B4310.

Four comfortable rooms are available to guests. The isolated position of this quiet village ensures a lack of the distractions normally associated with the regular tourist traps – a feature which many dedicated anglers will find most appealing. The hotel's public bar is a haunt of local farmers where gossip on matters agricultural is exchanged; and a convivial lot they are, too. A spacious beer garden looking out onto green fields provides a pleasant retreat to enjoy those last few drinks on a warm summer's evening.

The river is just under a mile away down a side road which takes one to the bridge marking the bottom boundary. A three-quarter mile stretch of right bank is offered to residents, some of which is in a wooded gorge where deep rock pools and rapids provide a wealth of good salmon lies. It is advised to carry a telescopic landing net here to avoid the sweating rage which inevitably follows a lost specimen fish. The upper part of the stretch is more open with lower banks. There are many gravel-lined shallows and tails of pools where shoals of sea-trout congregate after dusk.

Half and full-day tickets are on offer which can also be purchased by non-residents. Tickets are an additional charge on accommodation. All legal methods of fishing are allowed and good runs of migratory fish can be expected from quite early in the season given suitable river-flow conditions. A detailed map of the waters is on display in the public bar.

For a peaceful stay in a truly rural Welsh setting, this is the place.

The Forest Arms Hotel, Brechfa, Carmarthenshire, SA32 7RA.
Tel: 01267 202339.

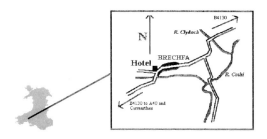

Gliffaes Country House Hotel

Not one, but *two* separate stretches of the famous River Usk to explore! In the prolific middle reaches too. If ever there was a must for the holiday angler, this is it.

Where? The Gliffaes Country House Hotel west of Crickhowell, standing in 33 acres of its own grounds a mile west of the A40. And the grounds are something special – a well-maintained mix of formal gardens, park and woodland containing many rare trees and shrubs.

The family-owned hotel suits its picturesque setting. Perched on a plateau about 60 feet above the Usk, it looks out over a wide vista of woods, fields and hills. There are 22 guest rooms on offer, all with private bath/shower. The bar, dining room and a spacious sun room all enjoy a view from the terrace to the hills beyond.

Facilities available to guests include a billiard room, tennis (hard court, practise wall and resident professional), putting (and golf practise net) and croquet. Equipment is available for all of these. Painters and bird watchers will find much to make a visit well worthwhile.

As for the fishing, one mile of left bank water is directly below the hotel while the other stretch is a little way upstream and consists of about three-quarters of a mile of double bank. Split into beats (2 rods per beat per day on a rotating basis) with the use of a comfortable fishing hut, the stretches include almost every type of water from deep pools to streamy runs. The average size of the wild brown trout is about 10 ounces with very many fish up to 2 lb or more. Salmon are present in the holding pools from early in the year.

Fly only is the rule except for salmon when spinning is also permitted at present. The fishing is an extra charge to accommodation. Dogs are not allowed in the hotel.

Early booking is essential for this deservedly popular fishing hotel.

The Manager, Gliffaes Country House Hotel, Crickhowell, Powys, NP8 IRH.
Tel: 01874 730371. *Fax:* 01874 730463.

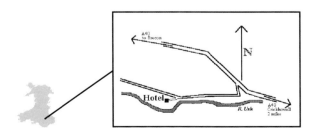

Gwydyr Hotel

Gethin's Bridge, Cottage, Barn, Beaver, Crooked, Fir Tree, Benson's, Oak and Willow Pools, as well as the famous Wall and Blue Pools, are just some of the excellent migratory fish venues on the River Conwy. They are all controlled by one of the best-known angling hotels in Wales – The Gwydyr.

For well over 100 years this fine establishment beside the A5 in Betws-y-coed has catered for visiting anglers. Many return year after year to this fishing Mecca at the gateway to Snowdonia and you can usually take your dog with you if you wish. 20 en suite bedrooms are offered, each with telephone and colour TV. The disabled can be accommodated and children are welcome.

Eight miles of first-class salmon and sea trout water is

offered on the rivers Conwy and Lledr split into two main beats; the lower Conwy section being over 2½ miles, two thirds of which is double bank, the rest being on the left bank. The river is wide here, flowing over gravel with some fine, large pools and runs.

The second stretch, double bank, starts from the Waterloo bridge and becomes steadily more bouldery upstream for about 1½ miles to the River Lledr junction. The Conwy holds some good brown trout, but strangely enough the Lledr is rather poor for this species. Nevertheless, the long stretch of left bank on this major tributary can produce really excellent salmon and sea trout from mid-year onwards.

Several miles of trout water on the Llugwy above the famous Swallow Falls and lake fishing is also available. Other beats and stretches can be arranged on request.

All legal baits are permitted except prawn. The well-stocked lounge bar or one of the several fishing huts provides a good setting to learn new excuses for an unjustifiably blank day or, alternatively, to show off your catch of silvery beauties.

For an enjoyable family holiday in truly beautiful surroundings with top-class fishing on the doorstep, the Gwydyr takes a lot of beating.

Gwydyr Hotel, Betws-y-coed, Gwynedd, LL24 0AB. *Tel:* 01690 710777. *Fax:* 01690 710777.

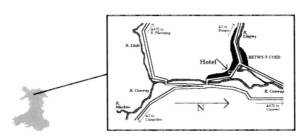

Lake Country House Hotel

Through a pleasantly green, leafy vale, the River Irfon bubbles and glides to its rendezvous with the Wye at Builth Wells. Rising from the high top of Bryn Garw just south of the Claerwen reservoir, it travels roughly south through a narrow ravine as far as the town of Llanwrtyd Wells, then east between rolling, pastured hills. Now among more gentle surroundings, it only has a few more miles to go before passing the renowned 3 red-star Lake Country House Hotel, a mile east of Llangamarch Wells.

Located at the mouth of a particularly beautiful wooded tributary valley, the elegantly-styled hotel overlooks the river about 100 yards away over well-tended lawns. Tall, handsome trees dominate much of the skyline giving an atmosphere of sanctuary to the immediate surroundings yet without the often accompanying feeling of isolation. A place to relax, indeed!

There are 19 bedrooms, 10 of which are part of full suites, and all are en suite. Accommodation and services are of a very high standard and two rooms are suitable for wheelchair users.

Guests are able to fish the best part of 2½ miles of the Irfon; a delightful river holding a large supply of brown trout, grayling to a very respectable size and salmon. Much of the stretch is situated on two great bends in the river, part of which is through a narrow, though easily accessible, section of the valley. Several species of coarse fish keep the salmonids and grayling company and large trout inhabit a 3 acre lake in the extensive grounds. A boat is available on this lake with gillie services provided on request and severely disabled anglers will find it quite easy to cast from the bank. The fishing is a modest extra charge on accommodation and reserved exclusively for guests. The only angling methods permitted are wet or dry fly.

Dogs are welcome to accompany guests in their rooms and the grounds.

Lake Country House Hotel, Llangamarch Wells, Powys, LD4 4BS.
Tel: 01591 620202. *Fax:* 01591 620457.

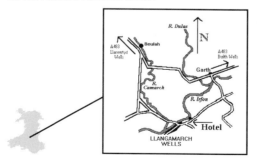

Lion Hotel

Although its course takes it mostly through the English countryside, the River Severn has its source and all its upper reaches in Wales. Here it is known as Afon Hafren. At the town of Llanidloes the Afon Clywedog joins on the left bank and the upper reaches of this major tributary stream have been dammed to form the reservoir of Llyn Clywedog, a noted angling centre for big trout.

A regulating reservoir, it releases water during times of drought, using the river as a pipeline for extraction further downstream. As can be imagined, such an activity can be a boon to anglers and fish alike during a hot, dry summer, when low water makes neighbouring rivers very difficult to fish.

Directly on the bank of the Severn, a few miles downstream, the Lion Hotel (WTB 3 crowns, highly commended) stands in the centre of Llandinam on the A470 about 7 miles west of Newtown. This pretty place is a "Best kept village in Wales" competition winner – and deservedly so. Five bedrooms are provided, one a "family room", and all are en suite. The large bar serves real ale but dogs are not allowed.

Nearly 4 continuous miles of the Severn, all both banks, can be fished here. Tickets are an extra charge on accommodation. The flat floor of the valley causes the river to constantly meander; deep pools on the bends contrasting with rippling runs and shallows over a gravel bed in the straighter stretches. A sparsely wooded area, much of the riverbank is open and clear of obstructions. Only fly fishing is permitted.

Grayling is the main quarry here. Trout are also present, but not in great numbers though some big specimens are said to lurk in the deeper pools. And salmon take a long time to run the full length of the Severn, arriving only late in the season. Nevertheless, the grayling fishing is superb with large shoals of very big fish found almost anywhere.

The Proprietor, Lion Hotel, Llandinam, Powys, SY16 5BY. *Tel:* 01686 688233.

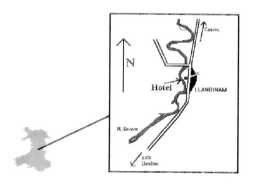

Llangoed Hall

The River Wye is justly considered by many to run in the most scenic valley in Wales. Not only this, but salmon catch returns prove this to be the most prolific, too. It is such a pity that hotels offering top-class accommodation together with good fishing are so rare on its banks.

But Llangoed Hall will satisfy even the most jaded of hotel visitors. A natural stone building of unsurpassed elegance, it stands on the valley floor well away from the A470 main road about a mile from the village of Llys-wen, south of Builth Wells. The rear of the hall, complete with heli-pad, looks out over flat green meadows to the river only a couple of hundred yards away.

The interior reflects the dignity of its outside elevations. Antiques abound in the high-ceilinged rooms and corridors.

The authentic atmosphere of the traditional country hall has been preserved with no regard to the cost but plenty for taste. Simply put, it is a pleasure to stay there.

There is an AA rating of 4 red stars with 1 Michelin star. All 23 beautifully-appointed bedrooms are en suite. Dogs are allowed by prior arrangement in the heated kennels. Many activities can be arranged given advance notice (clay pigeon shoots, archery, gliding, etc). A chauffeur-driven vehicle and butler service is offered.

The River Wye at this point is wide, strong in spate and an excellent mixture of very deep pools separated with runs studded with small islands and rock ledges across the flow of water. Just over a mile of right bank is exclusively available at an extra charge with an experienced gillie on call if required. A riverside hut provides shelter on wet days. Very good trout, plenty of salmon, grayling and shad besides other species of coarse fish (just have a look at the big stuffed pike mounted off the main hall) ensure that good fishing can be enjoyed all year round by any legal means.

Llangoed Hall, Llys-wen, Brecon, Powys, LD3 0YP. *Tel*: 01874 754525. *Fax*: 01874 754545.

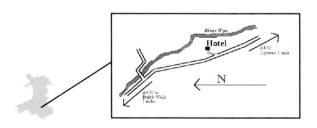

Penpont

More of a guest house than a hotel, this imposing family home offers four bedrooms and a large self-catering flat within the main house sleeping 12 people. The Doric-colonnaded house stands right by the river overlooking a sweeping lawn; the rest of the estate buildings reminding one of a tiny old-fashioned village.

The setting is superb and can truly be said to belong to another age although it is not far from the main A40, about half way between Brecon and Sennybridge.

Accommodation is mostly on a bed and breakfast basis but an evening meal can often be supplied by arrangement. No smoking is allowed in the bedrooms or dining room and the listed building is unfortunately not designed for the disabled requiring a wheelchair, having been built about 1666.

About a mile of the River Usk, nearly all double bank, belongs to the estate; a fine mixture of streamy runs, riffles and several deep salmon holding pools. Salmon can be caught here during the latter part of the season – from July on in a normal year – but it is for the trout fishing that most anglers will wish to return after sampling their first visit. The upper Usk provides arguably the most consistently good trout fishing anywhere in Wales – wild fish, too! Three-pounders are there to be caught and the evening rise in summertime has to be seen to be believed.

Only fly fishing is permitted. Four rods are offered at a charge of £10 per day (in 1998), payable as an optional extra for guests. Permits are only offered to others if not required by the guests.

Shady walks through the grounds under the magnificent old trees, a rose garden to sit in, plenty of natural wild life and a safe environment for children ensure the family is kept happy while you are down the river. Access to the water is satisfactory even for the relatively infirm.

To arrange for some trouting you will never forget, please contact:

Davina and Gavin Hogg, Penpont, nr Brecon, Powys, LD3 8EU. *Tel:* 01874 636202.

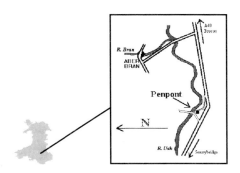

Rhuthun Castle

The site of this magnificent and internationally-renowned 3-star hotel has born witness to many important events in Welsh history. A *real* castle, reconstructed after nearly total destruction in 1647, it stands in the same spot as the original Welsh fortress which itself was rebuilt in 1296. Subjected to many acts of warfare and bloodshed (including a period under siege by Owain Glyndŵr and his wild-eyed, hairy horde) the castle now enjoys a more sedentary role as a venue for regular authentic mediaeval banquets (begun here in 1967) and high-profile conferences.

Although set within its own 30 acres of immaculate and quiet parkland, the hotel is only 3 minutes' walk from the central square of the ancient market town of Rhuthun. It offers 58 bedrooms of a very high standard, all en suite and all except one with private bath and shower. The single exception has a shower only. Dogs are not permitted.

The fishing available consists of approximately 12 miles mixed double and single bank on the river Clwyd and a major tributary called the Clywedog. All sorts of water are present – from long, calm pools to white torrents, deep and shallow. Much of the bank is wooded and wading is often necessary to fish many pools. Brown trout abound in both rivers; the Clwyd being stocked annually with 11-12 inch fish and the Clywedog preserved as a natural fishery. The Clwyd enjoys a consistently good run of salmon from fairly early in the season with the addition of shoals of sea trout after June in a year of normal rainfall.

The fishing is free to guests whatever their length of stay. All of the water mentioned is carefully managed by the Clwyd Angling Club and, as such, is not fully exclusive to the hotel. The number of club members is limited, however.

Even a full week is nowhere near long enough to properly fish all the fine water on offer. To ensure your place at this respected establishment, early booking is recommended.

The Manager, Rhuthun Castle, Rhuthun, Denbighshire, LL15 2NU.
Tel: 01824 702664. *Fax:* 01824 705978.

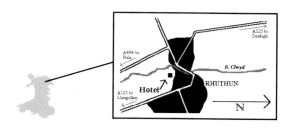

Severn Arms Hotel

Not near the River Severn as the name suggests, but right on the banks of the Ithon, a major tributary of the Wye. It is the largest building in the attractive little village of Penybont on the A44 north-east of Llandrindod Wells.

Besides the 10 bedrooms (all en suite) the 2-star and 3-crowns WTB-commended hotel contains an excellent restaurant and a large, well-appointed lounge bar. A traditional establishment, it provides a really comfortable environment while managing to avoid the glitz and flash of so many modern hotels. It is a perfect place for the true angler to feel at home but neither premises nor water is suitable for the severely disabled.

Dogs are allowed, there is real ale on tap and packed meals can be arranged. A detailed map of the waters is in the foyer.

The fishing comprises nearly 6 miles of water of which about half is double bank. Split into several beats, one long stretch immediately adjoining the hotel, the river can allow solitary and undisturbed fishing when required. Tickets are free to residents even if staying only one night and can also be purchased by non-residents.

A tranquil river, often winding between clay banks in this part of its course, the Ithon offers a pleasant mix of long, deep pools and gravelly riffles. It is an interesting place to fish as the surrounding countryside is completely rural with all the wildlife one could expect and no two parts of the river are similar. Fly only is the rule. Brown trout are in abundance, so are salmon later in the season, but it is the quality of the grayling which excels. Sizeable shoals of very large grayling or chub can often be spotted doing their mysterious rounds in the most unexpected locations. Other species of river coarse fish are also present.

All in all, the Severn Arms can be thoroughly recommended for an enjoyable angling holiday in both summer and winter.

The Severn Arms Hotel, Penybont, Llandrindod Wells, Powys, LD1 5UA.
Tel: 01597 851224 / 851344. *Fax:* 01597 851693.

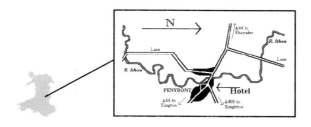

Tyddyn Llan Country House Hotel

On the edge of the pretty village of Llandrillo, in a section of the Dee valley known as the Vale of Edeyrnion, stands the Tyddyn Llan Hotel, a charming Georgian country house. At Corwen on the A5 trunk road, a turning south-west on to the B4401 will bring you to the location after a few miles.

Surrounded by well-tended gardens, attractive at any time of year, the low-profiled buildings contain not only a wealth of antique furniture but also one of the top restaurants in Wales. The marvellous menu has to be seen to be believed, many of the ingredients being grown on the premises in the hotel's own kitchen and herb gardens.

With a WTB rating of 4 crowns de luxe and 2 red AA stars, there are 10 bedrooms, all en suite; none of which, unfortunately, are accessible for wheelchairs. Guests' dogs are permitted in the rooms by prior arrangement and kennels provided.

Fishing can be enjoyed here all year. 4 continuous miles of the fabulous Dee, centred on Pont Cilan road bridge (double bank upstream, left bank downstream), are on offer exclusively to guests at a small extra charge. During the game fishing season, wild brown trout of a very respectable size can be sought in the gravelly runs and deep pools while salmon haunt the depths of the many named holding pools from about July onwards. A further boon is the fact that water let out of Llyn Celyn reservoir refreshes the river during the low-water months.

The Dee is a big, powerful and unspoilt flow of clean water and because of this chest waders are recommended to obtain the full benefit from this excellent stretch. Even more so in the winter months when great numbers of grayling (average size well over 1lb) are in their prime condition. All legal baits are allowed, fly being the first choice for grayling, naturally.

Fly fishing and tying lessons can be arranged with experienced gillies who will also accompany you on the river. Rough or driven shooting is often available.

Tyddyn Llan Country House Hotel, Llandrillo, nr Corwen, Denbighshire, LL21 0ST
Tel: 01490 440264. *Fax*: 01490 440414.

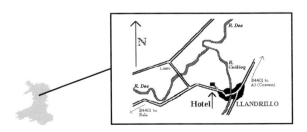

Ty'n-y-cornel Hotel

Possibly the oldest fishing hotel in the British Isles, the 2-star Ty'n-y-cornel at Tal-y-llyn Lake has welcomed anglers for about 150 years. Set in a sheltered corner at the lower end of the shallow 220 acre lake (Ty'n-y-cornel is Welsh for Corner House), it looks out upon a breathtaking view of Cader Idris mountain across the water.

The comfortable and well-appointed premises include a shop where fishing tackle can be bought or hired. Dogs are also permitted to accompany guests.

Severely disabled people in wheelchairs are able to be accommodated with a little assistance from a colleague. They can also partake in the fishing from various points about the lake or from a boat, if they are able.

Fishing concessions are extensive and encompass all types

of game fish. About 4½ miles, mostly double bank, of the River Dysynni are available in two beats of 2 and 2½ miles respectively. Salmon and sea trout run the river from May onwards and a sea trout of 16 lbs has been caught recently. In a wet year migratory fish will negotiate the attractive 9 mile river and enter Tal-y-llyn Lake from July. All legal forms of fishing are permitted on the small and prolific river but spinning in low water is frowned upon.

The whole of the lake is available from the bank or one of the fully-equipped hotel boats. Advance booking is advised and priority is given to full day lettings. Only artificial or natural fly is allowed.

The hotel can also provide fishing for truly wild trout at an altitude of 1,700 ft in one of the Pumlumon lakes – Llyn Bugeilyn (Shepherd's Lake). A boat is provided on this isolated wilderness water and artificial fly, or dapping with a natural one from a *drifting* boat, is the only method allowed.

All in all, the Ty'n-y-cornel can offer varied and very productive fishing in spectacular scenery which is also available to non-residents. The fishing is charged extra to accommodation.

Ty'n-y-cornel Hotel, Tywyn, Gwynedd, LL36 9A. *Tel:* 01654 782282. *Fax:* 01654 782679.

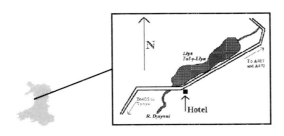

Ty'n-y-groes Hotel

West of the Arenig Mountains above Bala are many miles of high lumpy hills bordered on their western flanks by the valley of the Eden. This high, windswept region is the catchment area of Afon Mawddach; a wild, desolate moorland which provides all the local rivers with their distinctive peaty tints.

The Mawddach is joined by Afon Eden at the hamlet of Ganllwyd which straddles the A470 a few miles north of Dolgellau. Half a mile from the southern edge of this hamlet is located the 3-crown WTB-commended Ty'n-y-groes Hotel. It is also RAC acclaimed.

Sometimes mistaken to be a particularly pretty roadside public house, the Ty'n-y-groes is nevertheless a proper residential hotel and provides 8 comfortable rooms for the purpose (7 en suite, 1 single with private bath). Dogs are allowed to stay with guests at a small extra fee.

Directly over the road from the hotel a gate gives easy access down a path to the river. Although heavily wooded and flowing in a gorge at this point in its course, the Mawddach is a relatively friendly river to fish with some deep pools and powerful runs. Some nice residential trout are present but it is the quality of the migratory fish which attracts serious anglers. All legal methods are allowed.

Salmon and sea trout run the river from quite early in the year – a 17 lb sea trout was taken from this stretch in May 1995. There are 4 major holding pools and a multitude of other regular lies. The holdings are about 1¼ miles of right-hand bank and night fishing can be arranged – but take a good torch! It can get *very* dark down there in the gorge after the sun has set.

Four rods are allowed and there is an extra charge for the fishing. Guests have priority, of course. The hotel serves real ale in its very cosy lounge and packed meals can be provided.

The Landlord, Ty'n-y-groes Hotel, Ganllwyd, Dolgellau, Gwynedd. *Tel:* 01341 440275.

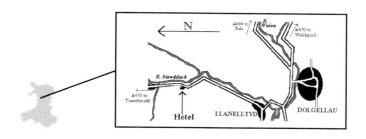

Usk Hotel

The River Usk has always been known for the excellent quality of its wild brown trout fishing – with salmon a close second. Sea trout don't appear to think much of it, though, except for one regular shoal. It appears in the waters owned by the Usk Hotel about the third week in July; fish up to 3lbs in weight jostling to share any available space with salmon and the teeming mass of indigenous wild brown trout.

This is a highly prolific section of the river.

Situated at the edge of the village of Talybont on Usk, this 3-crown (WTB) establishment has 12 bedrooms, all of which are en suite. From Crickhowell on the A40, travel about 9 miles in the direction of Brecon and watch carefully for the signposted turning to the left – it is an easy junction to miss. The hotel is on the valley floor at the entrance to the village after passing over the river.

Access to the water is easy, even for the disabled. One mile of left bank is available, consisting of typical Usk waterscape – wide, shallow runs and ripples where the trout go wild on the evening rise separated by the occasional deeper pool favoured by salmon.

Dogs are welcome at the hotel and packed meals can be provided for those reluctant to leave the river bank for feeding. Only fly fishing is permitted, wet or dry. Four rods per day are issued at an additional charge to accommodation and are available to day visitors; but resident guests have priority, of course. It is advised to book your preferred fishing times in advance to avoid disappointment.

Those of the gun persuasion may like to know that shooting (rough or party) can be arranged from the hotel. Again, prior booking is recommended.

This part of the Usk is considered by many to be one of the best in respect of the size of trout coupled with sheer numbers. Not to be missed!

The Usk Hotel, Talybont on Usk, Brecon, Powys, LD3 7EJ. *Tel:* 01874 676251.

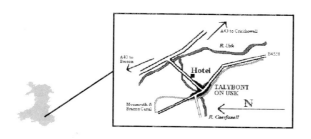

Lake Vyrnwy Hotel

With a 3-star rating (2 merits from the RAC for comfort and cuisine and 2 rosettes from the AA) together with a de-luxe grading from the WTB, this magnificent hotel must surely qualify as one of the top locations to stay in Wales.

Constructed at the same time as the huge dam holding back the waters of the River Vyrnwy (the late 1890s), the privately-owned hotel has the cosy atmosphere of a traditional country lodge. It is perched in a commanding position high above the dam with a panoramic view almost to the far end of the 1,100 acres of deep water. A spectacular position indeed!

There are 35 excellent bedrooms, all en suite with bath or shower. If you want a four-poster bed, you only have to ask! The kitchen garden in the grounds provides seasonal vegetables, edible flowers, herbs and fruit. Nearly all the food is home-made, even the mustards, chutneys, breads and preserves being created in the hotel kitchen. With wild mushrooms fresh from the fields and locally-gathered hedgerow fruits on the menu when available, the diet here must be the healthiest to be found anywhere.

Lake Vyrnwy (Llyn Efyrnwy in Welsh) has long been one of the top angling venues in the Principality. Regularly stocked with free-rising brown and rainbow trout, guests can fish the whole lake at an additional charge to bed and board. Only fly fishing from a boat is permitted but there are plenty of boats – and fish.

Free heated kennels are provided for guests' dogs and they are allowed in the bedrooms, though not in public rooms such as the lounges, restaurant, etc.

The 24,000 acres of hotel estate are plentifully occupied by all sorts of wildlife – including furred and feathered game. Shooting, both rough and driven, can be organised by prior arrangement.

Peace and freedom to roam are among the major attractions in this sparsely populated valley with its large RSPB reserve.

Lake Vyrnwy Hotel, Llanwddyn, Powys, SY10 0LY. *Tel:* 01691 870692. *Fax:* 01690 870259.

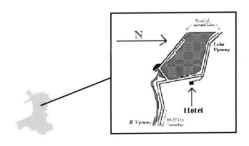

Other hotels offering fishing

THE *following hotels are those catering for anglers which either do not have such long stretches of water as those in the previous section and/or can arrange fishing on nearby waters which they do not themselves own. It must not be assumed that they are unsuitable for the holiday angler in any way whatsoever. The standard of service in all cases is remarkably high and visitors will find a friendly and traditional Welsh welcome on all their doorsteps.*

Black Lion Hotel

Llanybydder, Carmarthenshire, SA40 9UE. *Tel:* 01570 480242.

After 20 miles on the A485 north of Carmarthen, turn left on to the B4337 in the middle of Llanybydder and travel down a short hill. The hotel is on the left in the market square. Central position on the river bank and recently refurbished to a high standard. 5 en suite bedrooms. Fishing can be arranged for up to 3 miles of the Afon Teifi. Really excellent brown trout, salmon from mid-year on and the possibility of a grayling.

Bodfach Hall Hotel

Llanfyllin, Powys, SY22 5HS. *Tel:* 01691 648272. *Fax:* 01691 648272.

From Welshpool on the A483, head north-west for about 10 miles on the A490. The hotel is on the right (signposted) at the far end of the town and approached via a long driveway through open parkland. There are 9 en suite bedrooms. Dogs are allowed to accompany guests. The Afon Cain is close to its head-waters here, and only small, but is eminently suitable for catching the resident brook trout in some nice little pools with an outside chance of a grayling. About 300 yards of double bank are free to guests and further fishing can be arranged at Lake Vyrnwy not far away (at extra charge). Fly only.

Castell Elen Hotel

Dolwyddelan, Gwynedd, LL25 0EJ. *Tel:* 01690 750207. Beside the A470, 6 miles south-west of Betws-y-coed (A5).At the centre of the village only a stone's throw from the river. 2-star AA and 3-crowns WTB (highly recommended). There are 10 rooms, 7 of which are en suite. Bunkhouse accommodation sleeping up to 18 guests is available at extremely competitive rates. The fishing offered is free to guests even if only staying for one night. It consists of the right bank of a salmon-holding pool above the village bridge (the Afon Lledr is a marvellous sewin and salmon river from June onwards in a normal year) as well as a small lake about a mile into the mountains containing brown and rainbow trout together with some tench and carp. All legal methods are allowed. Night fishing is catered for and dogs are allowed on the premises. This is a real-ale hotel.

Castell Cidwm Hotel

Betws Garmon, Caernarfon, Gwynedd, LL54 7YT.
Tel: 01286 650243.   *Fax:* 01286 650243.
Close to the right-hand side of the A4085 about 8 miles south-west of Caernarfon. On the shore of Llyn Cwellyn facing across to the rugged majesty of Mynydd Mawr (Big Mountain). 3-crowns WTB – Highly Recommended. Eight rooms, all en suite. The fishing, half of the lake and fly only, is free to guests with no minimum stay required. Boats available.

Cothi Bridge Hotel

Pontargothi, Carmarthen. *Tel:* 01267 290251.
Located where the A40 crosses the noted Afon Cothi about 6 miles west of Carmarthen. 10 rooms. Caters for disabled anglers. 3-star commended. Packed meals and real ale. Nice bar overlooking the lower reaches of the river. Lawns to the river bank and a short stretch for the use of guests. More fishing can be arranged locally.

Crown Inn

Llanfihangel Glyn Myfyr, Cerrigydrudion, Denbighshire, LL21 9UL. *Tel:* 01490 420209.

From Cerrigydrudion on the A5 travel 3 miles east-north-east along the B5105. Small rural village setting, right on river bank. 3 rooms; comfortable but simple accommodation. Dogs are allowed and real ale is there to be quaffed. Guests may enjoy free fishing on more than 2 miles of the Afon Alwen; a dam-fed stream often giving good flows even during summer droughts. Mostly brown trout to a very decent size and it's full of them.

Dolbrodmaeth Inn

Dinas Mawddwy, Machynlleth, Powys, SY20 9LP. *Tel:* 01650 531333. *Fax:* 01650 531339.

About half way between Machynlleth and Dolgellau travelling north on the A470, look out for this attractive hotel on the left a little less than a mile after the roundabout at Mallwyd and just before the entrance to the woollen mill by the river bridge. 3-crowns WTB rating. 6 recently refurbished en suite rooms at present with another two available shortly. Dogs by arrangement. 2 rooms on the ground floor are suitable for wheelchair disabled. Real ale. Half a mile both banks of the Dyfi with three good holding pools free to guests only, even if staying just for one night. No bait restrictions. Also has two tickets for the use of guests on large stretches of the Wnion and Mawddach. Night fishing catered for.

Eagle Hotel

New Radnor, Powys, LD8 2SN. *Tel:* 01544 350208. *Fax:* 01544 350401.

About 6 miles west of Kington on the A44, the main road by-passes the village of New Radnor. If travelling westwards, take the first turning to the right into the old road and the Eagle (WTB 1 crown) will be seen on the right just before the village centre. There are 8 rooms (3 en suite) one of which is a dormitory room. It is a free house with real ale. Dogs are welcome. Close to the head-waters of Summergil Brook, a tributary of the River Lugg running in a deep, narrow valley, the hotel can offer about three quarters of a mile double bank fishing for small brook trout with the faint possibility of a grayling. This is free to guests. Access to beats on the Wye, Teme and Usk can be arranged at an extra charge. Other activities catered for and which can be arranged by the hotel are canoeing, caving, climbing, pony-trekking, paragliding, quad biking and many others.

Glanyrannell Park Country House Hotel

Crug-y-bar, Llanwrda, Carmarthenshire, SA19 8SA.
Tel: 01558 685230.   *Fax:* 01558 685784.
From Llandeilo on the A40, travel north on the B4302 for 9 miles to the village of Crug-y-bar. The hotel is signposted to the left as you enter the village. 2-star AA and 3-crowns Welsh Tourist Board (highly recommended). A truly rural location in 23 acres of attractive parkland. There are 8 rooms available, all en suite, plus a comfortable annexe of three units suitable for the extensively disabled with some assistance. Fishing (at an additional charge) arranged on many stretches of the Rivers Cothi, Towy and Teifi – a mixture of private and club waters to suit all tastes and pockets. Night fishing is catered for and dogs are welcome.

Glynwern Guest House

Llanilar, Aberystwyth, Ceredigion, SY23 4NY. *Tel:* 01974 241203.
At Llanfarian, 3 miles south of Aberystwyth, take the A485 towards Tregaron. Travel nearly 4 miles to Llanilar. Just after

entering the village look for a yellow sign on the left directing you down a narrow lane to the house. It is the first one of an attractive semi-detached pair on the right immediately after passing over the river bridge. A guest house, *not* a hotel, and very homely. 3 single rooms and 1 double. Two are en suite. There is no bar but a good pub is only a short distance away. Dogs are not allowed. The 30 miles of free fishing begin a few steps from the door at the bottom of the lawn. The Afon Ystwyth has a very good run of salmon and sea trout for which night fishing can be arranged, besides an excellent stock of brownies. All legal baits are permitted.

Hand Hotel

Llanarmon Dyffryn Ceiriog, nr Llangollen, Denbighshire, LL20 7LD. Tel: 01691 600262.   Fax: 01691 600262.
From the village of Chirk on the A5 (about 6 miles south-west of Llangollen), take the B4500 westwards and travel for about 9 miles. The hotel is facing you as you come over the village river bridge. An attractive 16th century building, 4-crowns WTB highly recommended, located in the quiet village square. Of the 14 en suite rooms, 2 are suitable for guests confined to a wheelchair and a large suite is also available. Fishing can be arranged in local pools and rivers at an extra charge. Catering is of a very high standard and the premises are fully licensed with a wide selection of wines lurking in a well-stocked cellar.

Hand Hotel

Llangollen, Denbighshire, LL20 8PL. Tel: 01978 860303. Telex: 61160.
Located in town centre. 3-star with 58 bedrooms (21 singles, 9 doubles, 22 twins and 6 triples). All en suite. Free fishing from

the rose garden in front of the hotel. About 100 yards of a first class run and pool on the River Dee with brown trout, salmon and grayling. Other coarse fish are present.

Horseshoe Inn

Llanyblodwel, Shropshire, SY10 8NQ. Tel: 01691 828969. From the A483 between Oswestry and Welshpool take the A495 westwards and after 2 miles continue west on the B4396. Take the first turning left (on a right-hand bend by a phone box) and this lane will take you into the village. Not *strictly* in Wales but *almost*. The village name is indisputably Welsh. Too good to leave out, anyway. A really charming old half-timbered early-15th century inn right on the river bank. 1 twin room (not en suite) and one "family" room with wash and shower. Just over a mile of right bank of the Afon Tanat, providing some excellent trout and grayling fishing. One-and-a-half pounders are very common. Late summer salmon to be found in several deep holding pools. Fly only and 3 rods per day limit.

The Lion Hotel

Llanbister, Llandrindod Wells, LD1 6TN. Tel: 01597 840244. The village of Llanbister lies approximately 10 miles north of Llandrindod Wells on the A483 at the junction with the B4356. The red-brick hotel is located on a knoll overlooking the river only 100 yards away at the entrance to the village. 4 rooms are on offer, 2 en suite, together with a self-contained flat sleeping 4 people which is suitable for the disabled (but phone to check on this). Nearly a mile of continuous, meandering (plenty of attractive corner pools) double-bank fishing on the upper River Ithon is free to guests, but unfortunately unsuitable for the wheelchair-bound. Wild brown trout are to be caught by fly only and there is no minimum stay to qualify for the free fishing. There is real ale on tap, packed meals available and dogs are allowed to accompany guests.

Mount Garmon Hotel

Holyhead Road, Betws-y-coed, Conwy, LL24 0AN. *Tel:* 01690 710335. *Fax:* 01690 710335.
A small, neat, family-owned hotel in an early Victorian house near the centre of the village. A high standard of accommodation is to be found in the 7 bedrooms, all en suite. About a quarter of a mile of the left bank of the famous Church Pool on the Afon Conwy is on offer (at an extra charge) only a few minutes' walk away; a salmon and sewin-holding stretch with a good run and eddy at the top. All legal methods are permitted. Night fishing is catered for and pets are welcome by prior arrangement.

Penmaenuchaf Hall Hotel

Penmaenpool, Dolgellau, Gwynedd, LL40 1YB.
Tel: 01341 422129. *Fax:* 01341 422129.
When eastbound on the A470 Dolgellau bypass, turn left on to the A493 and watch out for the hotel sign on the left after about half a mile. An idyllic setting on a small plateau overlooking the top of the Afon Mawddach estuary and the mountains to the north among 21 acres of very well kept gardens and ancient woodland. With a 3 star AA rating (plus 2 rosettes) and WTB 3 crowns (de-luxe), the hotel offers 14 quality rooms, all en suite. Four rods, free to guests, are retained on 13 miles of the rivers Mawddach and Wnion (excellent salmon and sea-trout water) and lake fishing for trout. There is no minimum length of stay to benefit from the

free fishing (subject to availability) and night fishing can be catered for by arrangement.

Peterstone Court

Llanhamlach, Brecon, Powys, LD3 7YB. *Tel:* 01874 665387. *Fax:* 01874 665376.

Travelling northwest on the A40 from Crickhowell, look out for the hotel sign on the left in the tiny village of Llanhamlach about 4 miles before Brecon. Twelve en suite bedrooms with WTB 5 crowns de luxe, and well-deserved. Rural setting by the river Usk with many extras to be enjoyed – a leisure suite, sauna and spa bath, outdoor heated swimming pool, solarium, croquet lawn and putting green, mountain bikes. Arrangements made for shooting and free passes for the local golf club. Two rods on half a mile left bank of the Usk for excellent wild trout and the occasional salmon are exclusively available at an extra charge. All legal methods allowed. Fishing can be arranged on many other rivers including the Towy and Teifi. Dogs allowed. Packed meals and real ale.

Plas Hall Hotel & Restaurant

Pont-y-pant, Dolwyddelan, nr Betws-y-coed, Conwy, LL25 0PJ. *Tel:* 01690 750206 / 306.   *Fax:* 01690 750526.

At the Waterloo Bridge on the A5 at Betws-y-coed take the A470 southbound in the direction of Blaenau Ffestiniog. After about 4 miles look out for the hotel sign on the left by Pont-y-pant railway station. Set in a particularly spectacular section of the Afon Lledr valley. Eighteen en suite rooms. Dogs are allowed. Several ground floor rooms suitable for the severely disabled. About 400 yards good salmon and sea trout fishing on the right bank free to guests – one large holding pool and rocky rapids with deep holes. Fly only, but worming is allowed on part of the stretch.

Royal Oak Hotel

High St, Llansanffraid Glynceiriog, Llangollen, Denbighshire, LL20 7EH. *Tel:* 01691 718243.

From the village of Chirk on the A5 (about 6 miles south-west of Llangollen), take the B4500 westwards and travel for about 5 miles. In the village centre at the middle reaches of the Afon Ceiriog, the hotel can offer 5 cosy rooms, none of which are en suite as yet. There is real ale and dogs are allowed by arrangement. Many stretches throughout the Ceiriog are available as well as an excellent beat on the Afon Alwen of 1¼ miles, mostly both banks. The fishing is fly only and free to guests, however short their stay. Salmon and good brown trout are in plentiful supply.

West Arms Hotel

Llanarmon Dyffryn Ceiriog, nr Llangollen, LL20 7LD. *Tel:* 01691 600665. *Fax:* 01691 600622.

From the village of Chirk on the A5 (about 6 miles South-West of Llangollen), take the B4500 westwards and travel for about 9 miles. The West Arms is the first building on the right over the river bridge at the beginning of the village. Located close to the upper reaches of the Afon Ceiriog, a tributary of the River Dee. About 1½ miles delightful double-bank small-stream trout fishing free to guests. Some surprisingly large fish in the deeper pools. Twelve en suite rooms are available, one of which is suitable for a wheelchair. Kennels are provided for dogs and there is real ale.

Hotels pleased to arrange Fishing

BELOW is a short list of Welsh hotels which, although having no water of their own or permanent arrangements with local angling clubs, are close (often very close) to good ticket water and are familiar with the prospects in their respective areas. They will always be pleased to arrange suitable fishing for their customers on request. All are patronised regularly by visiting anglers and are therefore used to the eccentricities of this particular species of sportsman (muddy boots and all). Enquirers are recommended to arrange their beats when booking, if necessary, in case there are only limited rods available.

Buckley Pines, Dinas Mawddwy, Machynlleth, Powys. Tel: 01654 531261. Conveniently placed for several migratory fish waters.

Cain Valley Hotel, Llanfyllin, Powys, SY22 5AQ. Tel: 01691 648366. Centrally situated in this charming little market town and convenient for a huge amount of ticket water on the Upper Severn, Vyrnwy, Banwy, Shropshire Union Canal and several big and small lakes.

Cawdor Arms Hotel, Llandeilo, Carmarthenshire, SA19 6EN. Tel: 01558 823500. Fax: 01558 822399. Close to middle reaches of River Towy. Very good salmon and sewin waters close by.

Eagles Hotel, Llanrwst, Conwy. Tel: 01492 640454. Town centre, right alongside the lower Conwy. Nearly a mile of club water within yards. Salmon, sewin and trout.

Emlyn Arms Hotel, Bridge Street, Newcastle Emlyn, Ceredigion. Tel: 01239 710317. 100 yards from very good lower Teifi ticket water. Salmon, sewin and brown trout.

Griffin Inn, Llyswen, Brecon, Powys, LD3 0UR. Tel: 01874 754241. Fax: 01874 754592. In middle Wye valley near good salmon, trout and grayling ticket water.

Lion Hotel, Berriew, nr Welshpool, Powys, SY21 8PQ. Tel: 01686 640452. Fax: 01686 640844. Plenty of ticket water on the prolific river Rhiw and the upper Severn with coarse fish in the nearby Shropshire Union Canal.

Nant Ddu Lodge Hotel, Cwm Taf, nr Merthyr Tudful, CF48 2HY. Tel: 01685 379111. Fax: 01685 377088. Between two well-stocked reservoirs with lots of local river and lake ticket water. Mostly trout.

Oak Tree Parc Hotel, Birchgrove Road, Skewen, Swansea, SA7 9JR. (By junction 44, M4). Tel: 01792 817781. Nicely situated to enjoy miles and miles of excellent ticket waters on the Tawe and Neath rivers. Brown trout and *plenty* of migratory fish.

Porth Hotel, Llandysul, Ceredigion, SA44 4QS. Tel: 01559 362202. The local club controls 26 miles of really good salmon, sewin and trout beats on the middle Teifi.

Tan-yr-onen Hotel, Beddgelert, Gwynedd. The clear waters of the river Glaslyn hold plenty of fine sewin and salmon from June on. Poor for trout, though.

Three Salmons Hotel, Bridge Street, Usk, Monmouthshire. Really good for large trout and salmon on the town ticket water.

White Lion Royal, 61 High Street, Bala, Gwynedd. Tel: Bala 520314. All of Bala Lake for coarse fish and miles of river ticket water on the upper Dee and tributaries for salmon, trout and grayling.

Ynyshir Hall, Eglwysfach, Machynlleth, Powys, SY20 8TA. Tel: 01654 781209. Fax: 01654 781366. Near lower River Dovey – famous for its sewin and with good salmon.

Facilities & concessions

FREE FISHING FOR GUESTS

Abernant Lake Hotel, Llanwrtyd Wells.
Bodfach Hall Hotel, Llanfyllin.
Bryn Howel Hotel, Llangollen.
Caer Beris Manor, Builth Wells.
Castell Cidwm Hotel, Betws Garmon.
Castell Malgwyn Hotel, Llechryd.
Crown Hotel, Llanfihangel Glyn Myfyr.
Dolbrodmaeth Inn, Dinas Mawddwy.
Dolmelynllyn Hall Hotel, Ganllwyd. (4 nights minimum
stay to qualify.)
Eagle Hotel, New Radnor.
Glynwern Guest House, Llanilar.
Hand Hotel, Llangollen.
Lion Hotel, Llanbister.
Plas Hall Hotel, Dolwyddelan.
Royal Oak Hotel, Glyn Ceiriog.
Ruthin Castle Hotel, Rhuthun.
Severn Arms Hotel, Pen-y-bont.
West Arms Hotel, Llanfair Dyffryn Ceiriog.

DOGS ALLOWED

*Some hotels will have certain restrictions or kennels provided.
Others only allow dogs by prior arrangement. Please check when
booking to ascertain what freedom of movement your pet will
have.*

Abernant Lake Hotel, Llanwrtyd Wells.
Bodfach Hall Hotel, Llanfyllin.
Brigands Inn, Mallwyd. (Kennels provided.)
Bryn Howel Hotel, Llangollen.
Caer Beris Manor, Builth Wells.

Cammarch Hotel, Llangamarch Wells.

Castell Elen Hotel, Dolwyddelan.

Castell Malgwyn, Llechryd, Cardiganshire.

Crown Inn, Llanfihangel Glyn Myfyr.

Dolbrodmaeth Inn, Dinas Mawddwy.

Dolmelynllyn Hall, Ganllwyd. (In 2 rooms only.)

Eagle Hotel, New Radnor.

Gwydyr Hotel, Betws-y-coed.

Glanyrannell Park Hotel, Crug-y-bar.

Hand Hotel, Llanfair Dyffryn Ceiriog. (By arrangement.)

Lake Country House Hotel, Llangamarch Wells.

Lion Hotel, Llanbister.

Llangoed Hall, Llyswen.

Mount Garmon Hotel, Betws-y-coed.

Peterstone Court, Llanhamlach, Brecon.

Plas Hall Hotel, Dolwyddelan.

Royal Oak Hotel, Glyn Ceiriog. (By arrangement.)

Severn Arms Hotel, Pen-y-bont.

Tyddyn Llan Country House Hotel, Llandrillo.

Ty'n-y-Groes Hotel, Ganllwyd. (Small daily fee.)

Ty'n-y-Cornel Hotel, Tal-y-llyn.

Usk Hotel, Talybont on Usk.

West Arms Hotel, Llanfair Dyffryn Ceiriog. (Kennels provided.)

WHEELCHAIR ACCESS TO HOTEL

Disabilities vary. Please check whether your individual requirements will be met before confirming a booking.

Abernant Lake Hotel, Llanwrtyd Wells.

Bryn Howel Hotel, Llangollen.

Caer Beris Manor, Builth Wells.

Dolbrodmaeth Inn, Dinas Mawddwy.

Glanyrannell Park Hotel. (With assistance.)
Gwydyr Hotel, Betws-y-coed.
Hand Hotel, Llanfair Dyffryn Ceiriog.
Hand Hotel, Llangollen.
Lake Country House Hotel, Llangamarch Wells. (2 rooms.)
Lion Hotel, Llanbister.
Plas Hall Hotel, Dolwyddelan.
Ty'n-y-Cornel Hotel, Talyllyn. (With assistance.)
West Arms Hotel, Llanfair Dyffryn Ceiriog. (1 room.)

WHEELCHAIR ACCESS TO FISHING

Abernant Lake Hotel, Llanwrtyd Wells. (Lake.)
Caer Beris Manor, Builth Wells. (Lake.)
Ty'n-y-Cornel Hotel, Talyllyn. (Lake and boats.)
Lake Country House Hotel, Llangamarch Wells. (Lake.)
Usk Hotel, Talybont on Usk, Brecon. (Riverbank.)

NIGHT FISHING ARRANGED

Brigands Inn, Mallwyd.
Castell Elen Hotel, Dolwyddelan.
Dolaucothi Arms Hotel, Pumsaint.
Dolbrodmaeth Inn, Dinas Mawddwy.
Dolmelynllyn Hotel, Ganllwyd.
Glanyrannell Park Hotel, Crug-y-bar.
Glynwern Guest House, Llanilar.
Gwydyr Hotel, Betws-y-coed.
Mount Garmon Hotel, Betws-y-coed.
Ruthin Castle Hotel, Rhuthun.
Ty'n-y-Groes Hotel, Ganllwyd.

FISHING RESERVED EXCLUSIVELY FOR GUESTS

Brigands Inn, Mallwyd.
Bodfach Hall Hotel, Llanfyllin.
Bryn Howel Hotel, Llangollen.
Caer Beris Manor, Builth Wells. (On own Irfon waters only.)
Dolbrodmaeth Inn, Dinas Mawddwy.
Glanyrannell Park Hotel. (Depending on location arranged.)
Gwydyr Hotel, Betws-y-coed. (Some beats.)
Lake Country House Hotel, Llangamarch Wells.
Llangoed Hall, Llyswen.
Peterstone Court, Llanhamlach, Brecon.
Tyddyn Llan Country House Hotel, Llandrillo.

FLY-ONLY RULE

Bell Hotel, Glangrwyne.
Bodfach Hall Hotel, Llanfyllin.
Bryn Howel Hotel, Llangollen.
Caer Beris Manor, Builth Wells. (Preferred on own Irfon waters.)
Cammarch Hotel, Llangamarch Wells.
Castell Cidwm Hotel, Betws Garmon.
Gliffaes Country House Hotel, Crickhowell.
Horeshoe Inn, Llanyblodwel.
Lake Country House Hotel, Llangamarch Wells.
Lion Hotel, Llanbister.
Lion Hotel, Llandinam.
Pen-pont, Brecon.
Royal Oak Hotel, Glyn Ceiriog.
Severn Arms Hotel, Pen-y-bont.
Ty'n-y-cornel Hotel. (on lake.)
Usk Hotel, Talybont on Usk.
West Arms Hotel, Llanfair Dyffryn Ceiriog.

LIMITED RODS WITH PRIORITY TO GUESTS

When arranging a booking at one of these hotels, don't forget to inform them about the days on which you wish to reserve a rod. Failure to do so could result in grievous disappointment if it is left until the last minute, only to find that the stretch is fully booked for that particular day when you change your mind and decide on an extra day's fishing. It has been observed that angling conditions are invariably perfect on such occasions.

Bell Hotel, Glangrwyne.

Caer Beris Manor, Builth Wells. (On Wye waters.)

Cammarch Hotel, Llangamarch Wells.

Gliffaes Country House Hotel, Crickhowell.

Glynwern Guest House, Llanilar.

Gwydyr Hotel, Betws-y-coed. (Some stretches.)

Horseshoe Inn, Llanyblodwel.

Pen-pont, Brecon.

Peterstone Court, Llanhamlach, Brecon.

Ty'n-y-groes Hotel, Ganllwyd.

Usk Hotel, Talybont on Usk.

Which waters for which hotels?

HERE is a guide for matching hotels mentioned earlier in the booklet with the rivers or lakes you wish to fish. The following waters are either owned by, close to – with regular access – or exclusive to the hotel indicated. An entry marked with ** means that access can often be arranged to that water by the hotel indicated and there may be an extra charge for the permit (though not always). All lengths of water stated must be considered to be only approximate, but they give a good indication of what length is available.

AFON ALWEN

Crown Hotel, Llanfihangel Glyn Myfyr. Over 2 miles double bank.

Royal Oak Hotel, Glyn Ceiriog. 1¼ miles, mostly both banks.

AFON CAIN

Bodfach Hall Hotel, Llanfyllin. 300 yards both banks of brook.

AFON CAMARCH

Cammarch Hotel, Llangamarch Wells. About 3 miles.

AFON CEIRIOG

Royal Oak Hotel, Glyn Ceiriog. Many stretches, several miles total.

West Arms Hotel, Llanfair Dyffryn Ceiriog. 1½ miles double bank small stream.

AFON CLEIFION

Brigands Inn, Mallwyd. About ¾ mile.

AFON CLWYD

Ruthin Castle Hotel, Rhuthun. About 10 miles.

AFON CLYWEDOG (Tributary of Clwyd)

Ruthin Castle Hotel, Rhuthun. About 4 miles.

AFON CLYWEDOG (Tributary of Wnion)

Dolmelynllyn Hall Hotel, Ganllwyd. 1¼ miles double + ¾ right bank.

Dolbrodmaeth Inn, Dinas Mawddwy. 1¼ miles double + ¾ right bank.**

AFON CONWY

Gwydyr Hotel, Betws-y-coed. 4½ miles mostly double bank.
Mount Garmon Hotel, Betws-y-coed. ¼ mile left bank.

AFON COTHI

Cothi Bridge Hotel, Pontargothi. 150 yards left bank.
Dolaucothi Arms, Pumsaint. 8½ miles nearly all double bank.
Forest Arms Hotel, Brechfa. ¾ mile right bank.
Glanyrannell Park Hotel, Crug-y-bar. Various. Subject to availability.**

CREGENNEN LAKES

Dolmelynllyn Hall Hotel, Ganllwyd. 2 medium-sized lakes – one stocked.**

AFON DYFI (DOVEY)

Brigands Inn, Mallwyd. 1¾ miles mostly both banks.
Dolbrodmaeth Inn, Dinas Mawddwy. ½ mile both banks.

AFON DYFRDWY (DEE)

Bryn Howel Hotel, Llangollen. 5 miles.
Hand Hotel, Llangollen. 100 yards right bank.
Tyddyn Llan Country House Hotel, Llandrillo. 4 miles, half double bank, rest left bank.

AFON DULAS (Tributary of Irfon)

Cammarch Arms Hotel, Llangamarch Wells. 1 mile.

AFON DYSYNNI

Ty'n-y-cornel Hotel, Talyllyn. 4½ miles mostly double bank.

ELAN VALLEY RESERVOIRS

Elan Valley Hotel, Rhayader. 1,600 acres.

AFON GWY (WYE)

Caer Beris Manor, Builth Wells. 4 miles varying banks.
Eagle Hotel, New Radnor. Various.**
Elan Valley Hotel, Rhayader. 5 miles, mostly double bank.
Llangoed Hall, Llyswen. Over 1 mile right bank.

AFON HAFREN (SEVERN)

Lion Hotel, Llandinam. Nearly 4 miles double bank.

AFON IRFON

Abernant Lake Hotel, Llanwrtyd Wells. 1½ miles left bank.
Caer Beris Manor, Builth Wells. 1 mile including hotel's own
water of 1,000 yards.
Cammarch Arms Hotel, Llangamarch Wells. 3½ miles.
Lake Country House Hotel, Llangamarch Wells. 2½ miles.

AFON ITHON

Severn Arms Hotel, Pen-y-bont. Various stretches totalling 6
miles either bank.

AFON LLEDR

Castell Elen Hotel, Dolwyddelan. 100 yards left bank.
Gwydyr Hotel, Betws-y-coed. 3½ miles left bank.
Plas Hall Hotel, Dolwyddelan. 400 yards right bank.

AFON LLUGWY

Gwydyr Hotel, Betws-y-coed. Several miles mostly right bank.

LLYN ARLACH

Caer Beris Manor. Small put-and-take water.

LLYN BUGEILYN

Ty'n-y-cornel Hotel, Talyllyn. Wild mountain trout fishery.

LLYN CWELLYN

Castell Cidwm Hotel, Betws Garmon. Half of the lake.

LLYN CYNWCH

Dolmelynllyn Hall Hotel, Ganllwyd. Medium sized lake regularly stocked.

LLYN EFYRNWY (LAKE VYRNWY)

Lake Vyrnwy Hotel, Llanwddyn. 1,100 acres. Very well stocked.

LLYNGWYN

Elan Valley Hotel, Rhayader. Smallish lake. Put-and-take big trout.

LLYN TAL-Y-LLYN

Ty'n-y-cornel Hotel, Tal-y-llyn. 220 acres. Stocked with trout. Migratory fish later in year.

AFON MARTEG

Elan Valley Hotel, Rhayader. 3 miles double bank.

AFON MAWDDACH

Dolmeynllyn Hall Hotel, Ganllwyd. 1¾ miles left bank.
Ty'n-y-groes Hotel, Ganllwyd. 1¼ miles right bank.
Dolbrodmaeth Inn, Dinas Mawddwy. 1¾ miles left bank.**

SUMMERGIL BROOK

Eagle Hotel, New Radnor. ¾ miles double bank small
stream.

AFON TANAT

Horseshoe Inn, Llanyblodwel. Over 1 mile right bank.

RIVER TEME

Eagle Hotel, New Radnor. Various.**

AFON TEIFI

Black Lion Hotel, Llanybydder. Up to 3 miles.
Castell Malgwyn Hotel, Llechryd. 2¼ miles left bank.
Glanyrannell Park Hotel, Crug-y-bar. Various stretches
subject to availability.**

AFON TYWI

Glanyrannell Park Hotel, Crug-y-bar. Various stretches
subject to availability.

AFON TWRCH. (Tributary of Cothi)

Dolaucothi Arms Hotel, Pumsaint. ½ mile.

AFON TWYMYN

Brigands Inn, Mallwyd. 8 miles, mostly double bank.**

AFON WNION

Dolmelynllyn Hall Hotel, Ganllwyd. Stretches either bank totalling over 8 miles
Dolbrodmaeth Inn, Dinas Mawddwy. Stretches either bank totalling over 8 miles.**

AFON WYSG (USK)

Bell Hotel, Glangrwyne. 450 yards right bank.
Eagle Hotel, New Radnor. Various stretches.**
Gliffaes Country House Hotel, Crickhowell. 1 mile left bank + ¾ mile double bank.
Pen-pont, Brecon. Over 1 mile double bank.
Usk Hotel, Talybont on Usk. 1 mile left bank.

AFON YSTWYTH

Glynwern Guest House, Llanilar. 30 miles mostly both banks.

That's the lot!

So now please enjoy your holiday to the fullest

and

Good luck with the fishing!

By the same author ...

£6.95

Essential reading for all those keen game, coarse and sea anglers wishing to spend a carefree holiday in Wales.

Talybont, Ceredigion, Cymru SY24 5AP
e-bost ylolfa@ylolfa.com
y we http://www.ylolfa.com/
ffôn (01970) 832 304
ffacs 832 782
isdn 832 813